Pretty in A Hard Way

poems by

Michelle Brooks

Finishing Line Press
Georgetown, Kentucky

Pretty in A Hard Way

ACKNOWLEDGMENTS

I'd like to thank my family and friends, living and dead, without whom
this book would not exist. Listed in no particular order, I offer my deepest
gratitude to Beth Brooks, Angela Bills, Emily Quane, Hank Ballenger, Brad
Foster, Don and Margie Brooks, Marci Anderson, Trent Vanegas, Black Cat
Press, Linda and Jim Mueller, Laura and Pinkney Benedict, Shawn Behlen,
Sharon Serra, Robin Konarz, my Detroit friends (Stacey, Jodi, Mark, Tim),
Ken Mandel, Barb, Vickie, Linda, Jamie, Donna Ballenger, Peter and Connie,
Dominic Baffo, Deacon John at St. Sylvester's, Daniel Mueller, and all those
people who have supported and loved me, too numerous to mention. Thanks
to all the journals that published these poems and to Finishing Line Press for
accepting this manuscript. And thanks to Saint Jude, who never fails.

Publisher: Leah Maines
Editor: Christen Kincaid
Cover Art: Michelle Brooks
Author Photo: Beth Brooks
Cover Design: Elizabeth Maines McCleavy

Printed in the USA on acid-free paper.
Order online: www.finishinglinepress.com
        also available on amazon.com

Author inquiries and mail orders:
Finishing Line Press
P. O. Box 1626
Georgetown, Kentucky 40324
U. S. A.

Table of Contents

If You're Drinking to Forget, Please Pay in Advance 1

Imprisoned Lightning 2

Enchantment Ballroom 3

Smart, Very Smart 4

Strike Anywhere 5

Applebee's Hotel Bar—Boca Raton, Florida 6

That's Not A Window, It's A Mirror 7

The Saint of This Used to Be 8

Three Mile Island at Night 9

The Bride of Frankenstein 10

This Needs to Look Like an Accident 11

The Kitchen Is Closed but the Bar Stays Open Late 12

Vision 13

San Francisco, Dusk, Pre-Millennium 14

The Bronx Is Burning 15

San Francisco, Dusk, Pre-Millennium 16

Watch What Develops 17

Where Good Things Come Easy 18

Esoterica 19

Flamethrower 20

If I Seem Free, It's Because I'm Always Running 21

The Priestess of the Imperial Cult 22

The Year in Review 23

Possum Kingdom Lake 24

The Judgment of Heaven 25

Stock Footage 26

Obituary for A Neon Angel 27

Blank Inside for Your Message 28

Walk-In Emergencies Welcome..29

Overheard, or This Is Not *Nighthawks*...30

Arson...31

Half-Life..32

Look What You Created 33

Color Your World...34

Stop Me If You've Heard This One Before..35

The Arsenic Hour 36

How to Make Your Own Bed 37

Endless Summer 38

In the Terminal 39

The Lady or the Tiger? Capture Them Both 40

Obey the Night...41

This Painting Is Part of Our Permanent Collection.........................42

I Am the Fist 43

Exclusions May Apply..44

You Are the Camera 45

Where the Negatives Are Buried..46

Trick and Treat...47

Take, Lock, and Hide 48

Straight No Chaser 49

Vacation Bible School 50

The City of God 51

These Streets...52

Pretty in A Hard Way...53

At the Crossroads of the Dying World 54

The Show Must Go On 55

This book is dedicated to Shawn Behlen.

"We hope for better things; it will arise from the ashes"
("*Speramus meliora; resurget cineribus*")

Motto of Detroit, Father Gabriel Richard, 1805

If You're Drinking to Forget, Please Pay in Advance

I am the last drink of the night, the one
you shouldn't have. I don't wish you
harm. My enemies have abandoned
me. A man offers to buy me a drink, asks
What's your poison? I am the poison, but
I keep that to myself and smile. One drink
never hurt anyone, right? Still, I hesitate,
listening to sirens attend to someone else's
emergency. Who knows if I have come
to this place for a moment such as this.

Imprisoned Lightning

The Statue of Liberty crosses Nine Mile, smoking
a cigarette, a sign for some off-brand tax service
tethered around his neck as I drive in the early morning
hours, the tattered end of winter, all gray snow lining
the edges. At the red light, I notice a health food store,
a handmade sign in the window that says, *Disease starts
in the Colon*, a video rental store, closed for good.
On many Friday nights, I rented their movies about people
I will never know, places to which I won't travel.
The Statue of Liberty grinds out his butt on the sidewalk,
and raises his torch, ready to resume his duties while
my life is lodged somewhere inside me, a sliver of glass
I can't remove. The poor, the tired, the huddled, they are
all here like me, without a golden door, only matches
from places that no longer exist and yet refuse to burn.

Enchantment Ballroom

A friend tells me he is not
himself these days. I pause
and think about how I longed
to be someone else for years—
composed and poised, someone
who didn't always have a hair
out of place, someone who knew
the secrets of the world. And I
think of a girl named Movanna
who told me that she'd do anything
to be beautiful like me. Her last
name was Lack. She's dead now.
And I'm still myself. Strange.
Do you think our lives would be
different if we were the kind
of people who took dance lessons?
you ask as we pass a storefront
with the words Enchantment
Ballroom etched above the awning,
illustrated with a clip art of a woman
and man locked in an embrace. Were
the clip art couple married or merely
bound together by circumstance? I
tell him, *I guess we'll never know.*

Smart, Very Smart

Jimmy Carter looked green
as he delivered his last state
of the union. Of course, everyone
did on the old Magnavox for ten
minutes or so. My parents turned
it on well advance of the buyer
who had called in response
to the Thrifty Nickel ad. *It takes
a few minutes to get going*, my dad
said. *Don't we all?* the man replied,
broken vessels on his nose, a map
that led nowhere. My mother forced
a smile and offered coffee. *I'll take it,*
the man said. *And the coffee too.*

Jimmy spoke of malaise a crisis
of confidence as my dad unplugged
him and offered to load the television
into the man's car. My mom looked
relieved. We needed the money. We
always did. *Thank you. That guy
depresses me*, the man said. *Tell me
something I don't know, Jimmy.* His hands
shook when he picked up the mug.
*Hell, no matter who you pick, they're
all disappointing*, the man said, *once
the bloom is off the rose.* He swilled
the last of his coffee like it was medicine,
the kind you forced yourself to take even
though it didn't work so well anymore.

Strike Anywhere

Nothing bad can happen.
Now you're waiting for it,
right? Wait all you want. No
one is coming home. When
trouble masquerades as solace,
when a room speaks once
and tells all before it closes up
and obliterates you with noise
to subtract from what you already
know, when you forget where I am,
I will uncover the negatives
you hid. You can't see me yet.
I am a necklace you can't untangle,
a knife waiting for someone's neck.

Applebee's Hotel Bar—Boca Raton, Florida

A man walks into a bar.
He tells me this isn't a joke,
that he wants to obliterate
the past week. The week no
longer exists except in himself
so that's where he begins. He
forgoes the chicken quesadillas
for shot after shot of Jim Beam.
He means business. I don't know
what went wrong and before
long, neither does he. He's not
from here. None of us are. This
is the river from which we drink
and wonder how we can sing
the songs of Zion in a foreign
land. People call this place God's
waiting room, but isn't everywhere?

That's Not A Window, It's A Mirror

My darkness may include unwanted
side effects like dizziness and shortness
of breath. Imagine my hands around your
throat. Stop immediately if thoughts
of suicide worsen. I am contraindicated,
for people with certain underlying conditions.
Off-label, take me as needed for pain. My
label doesn't specify which kind. After all,
pain is information that nobody wants.
Severe side effects, including death, may
occur. Stop using me and seek immediate
medical attention for uncontrollable movements
which can be permanent. Don't act surprised.
After all, you knew I came with a warning label.

The Saint of This Used to Be

I didn't know any better except to love
it, the bluish glow of televisions at night,
snow that fell like promises only to
turn dirty and gray, like the city itself.
The landlords told us that this used
to be paradise while I watched
a neighbor choke his daughter. *Bitch,*
he yelled, *this is your last chance.*
The streets in the city changed named
halfway, leaving me wonder what
miracle or wonder might happen next.

Three Mile Island at Night

I am waiting for the disaster of my
life to reveal itself. All the elements
are present for an accident of serious
consequence. When it does, I will make
the oldest wish—for things to be as they once
were, the moment before the inevitable.
First pretend this isn't happening. If you
don't acknowledge it, it will go away. It's
a bad dream. When you can no longer hide
it, shift blame. Wash your hands. Rinse,
lather, repeat. The poison has seeped into you.
You are Cassandra. You told everyone, and now
you and your crystal ball can't be blamed.
You saw this happening. You knew. Or you
didn't. You had no idea. You can't be blamed.

At night there is no difference between you
made a mistake and *you are a mistake*. Make
no mistake now—you are here with no map.
Hell is a self-perpetuating circle. You aren't
going anywhere. That was before, the moment
you can't conjure. Make no mistake. You are home.

Bride of Frankenstein

She's a hard-drinking divorcee, I imagine,
childless. Her friends speculate that she
never met the right man. At the boutique,
the girls ooh and aah as they try on dress
after dress, saying, *It's my big day. It has
to be perfect.* She adjusts straps, tells them
they look beautiful. It's not a lie when
you say it about brides and babies. Still, it
takes its toll. After work, she comes home
to her rented upper flat and smokes alone
on the balcony. *You have to put yourself
out there*, they say. They tell her to lower her
standards. She nods and tilts her head, blows
a smoke ring into the fading daylight. She
doesn't begrudge these telephone sages, but
she's decided the cooling board suits her. *I need
to get ready for work*, she tells them. *This beehive
doesn't fix itself.* She lays out her bridal gown
for work tomorrow, half-listening. They try to fix
her up. After their tepid descriptions, she demurs.
They lose patience. *Don't fool yourself. Nobody's
perfect.* You don't have to tell me, she thinks.
It's not like I haven't seen some real monsters.

This Needs to Look Like an Accident

A woman on a commercial once told me,
Don't hate me because I'm beautiful.
I forget the product or the why beauty
should inspire hate. Much easier to loathe
myself, the legion of flaws, the persistent
sabotage I used as a repellant against getting
what I wanted. Easier to pretend I never
wanted anything than to give admittance
to the sorrow of disappointment. Easier
to pretend I wasn't hungry when all the cake
was gone. Easier to act as if I meant to do
the thing I did not want to do. If you are
inclined to hate me, don't bother. I'll pretend
not to notice or act like your hate is something
else. Surprised? You shouldn't be. It's not like
I promised to keep my eyes on my own paper.

The Kitchen Is Closed but the Bar Stays Open Late

On daytime television shows, the fog
telegraphs that it's all a dream. I only
know there's a car. It runs on blood, but
I wake up before I give enough to drive.
Awake, I'm always later than I think.
It's always a full moon. Sirens wail. Neon
glows. This world full of these splashes
of noise and color only says, *Keep going.*

Vision

My mother always made burning
bushes for parties, thin deli
meat with cream cheese frozen
and then cut into circles. If God
spoke from these appetizers what would
He say to the gathered faithful, the guests
attempting to find solace in Wild Turkey
and Blue Nun? As a child I passed around
the offerings until the plate was empty,
like a desert before the promised land.

San Francisco, Dusk, Pre-Millennium

A hint of shadow crosses your face,
the headlights from oncoming cars
washes over us as the day leeches away.
Our hearts beat behind bullet-proof glass,
sealed off for no one's protection, preventive
measures taken only after the house has
been looted. We visited the Camera Obscura
today, and I looked through the pinhole,
unsure of how it worked and only saw my own
eyelashes instead of the beach. The waves crash
against the shore, and it gets late. People come
home from work. We keep walking, telling each
other we have all the time in the world, that we
have no place to be, that it's not as late as it seems.

The Bronx Is Burning

The rain falls in sheets
and the ground rises like
a fist. There's this past, you
see, most of which I will take
to my grave as have others
before me. What would I have
done if I knew the ending
would come so soon? Would
love flicker behind my almost
dead eyes? Or would I still
conceal everything I didn't want
you to know and catch my death,
just like everyone said I would?

Watch What Develops

I have never been to Coney Island
yet the Ferris wheel in sepia-drenched
pictures, the greenish tint of old Polaroids,
the relics rendered in black and white
fills me with a past I will never know.
And yet it is mine, a ghost that speaks
my name as if I'd been there, haunted
by rides I never took, the fun I never had.

Where Good Things Come Easy

Forget about your change.
You don't need it. You are
under the neon night sky. This
is all yours—the sidewalk
lined with winners of the race
to the bottom. Count yourself
among their ranks. You squeeze
past them, people huddled together,
sharing the same cigarette. A tiny
flag floats in the gutter, adorned
with a tag that tells you how your
donation will help the wounded
veterans. Any amount is appreciated.
Walking away from the Seven-Eleven,
you stare up at the starless sky. No matter
what you do, you can't move the clouds.

Esoterica

My mother's friend cut open
snakes to read the future,
an ancient divination ritual,
haruspicy. Everyone tells
me I've seen some weird shit. I
don't disagree. After she sliced
open the snake, the friend smiled
and asked, *What have we here?*
before launching into a prophesy
of rocky love affairs, secrets concealed
so long only the body remembers.
I never learned to read the entrails,
but I know what the inside of a snake
looks like, a dead one, the kind some
people call the only good one.

Flamethrower

If I were a weapon, I'd be a Molotov
Cocktail, poised in the hand of a revolutionary.
Cheap and easy to make, I'd explode once,
sacrificing the container to set the known
world ablaze. And if I were a potion, I'd
be truth serum, and you'd tell me secrets
that you had concealed even from yourself.
I'd infect your blood with the promise
of liberation. And if I were a plant, I'd be
Poison Hemlock streaked with purple
and red. Who knows? Maybe you'd pick
me, mistaking me for something harmless.

If I Seem Free, It's Because I'm Always Running

for James Gandolfini

In my dreams, were are somewhere between
Saturday night and Sunday morning. Places
start to close, and yet we are not done. You
are never ready to go home because nothing
can fill the longing for streetlights, for another
drink, for sirens, for another tale from the city.
We take a last chance power drive, Bruce wailing
on the radio. I am a passenger in this darkness
on the edge of town. Who cares if this is the road
less travelled? It's a road, and we rush down
it because there is no drink that can cap the night,
no goodbye that doesn't feel like it might be the last.

The Priestess of Imperial Cult

Time runs through my hands
and I arrange myself around it.
The moments die around me.
I don't cause death. Witness my
composure. I don't blink. Lives
shatter, stars die, ground shifts.
I don't forget what used to be even
as the future stretches like a promise
of something you will love when
really you don't feel anything except
your heart pierced when you know
nothing lasts. Don't tell me you know
better. I lived here before you did.

The Year in Review

Bullets flew from witnesses' mouths,
telling of near misses, of the fallen
who surrounded them. The fallen live
in slideshows, as if machines had become
ghosts, promising to haunt us on an endless
loop. We try to make sense of it all, but
the story goes everywhere and nowhere.
The snake eats its tail and remains whole.
What does it all mean? We can only watch.

Possum Kingdom Lake

I'd play in the water while the adults drank
and talked about the veil between the worlds,
the ones to whom they'd said their goodbyes.
Now I see them only in dreams, the dead,
the vanished, and nobody remembers those days,
the distant shore and turning from it, the lost
kingdom of adults. These days, nobody carries
me to the backseat where I once feigned sleep,
dreaming of other lives, a luxury I had when someone
else, no matter how unsteady, was at the wheel.

The Judgment of Heaven

Let's start with this—

There is no one here
to save you. The bar closed
hours ago, and the wind
cuts through your coat.
You are the decoration
for a party that is over,
the opposite of anticipation.
You can't avoid it anymore.
What will rinse the blood
off your hands? If only the ads
were true, if only someone
sold a product that could get
the tough stains out, if only
you could make yourself look
like nothing ever happened.

Stock Footage

You meet someone who asks, *Are
you free?* A question like a gun,
loaded. When you learned to shoot,
your instructor told you not to put
your finger on the trigger until you
intended to pull it, the assumption being
that you would. Is this the answer
to the question your life asks no matter
how hard you try to muffle it? You buy
yourself some time. You pick a letter,
any letter, but you see nothing except
pages filled with your own handwriting.

Obituary for A Neon Angel

The city, alive with sirens, makes you
long for other days, for the lost ones.
The causalities of your youth stay hidden,
buried beneath the darkness you cast
in every direction. The night casts its own
shadows onto your small stake of the known
world. *If you love me, you will tell me your
whole heart,* you whispered to various men,
not knowing that diminishment seeps
into everything around it. You become
a crime scene, the tape around a body long
removed, all color drained by morning.

Blank Inside for Your Message

You are free to say anything.
Of course, it can and will be held
against you. You should know
the rules before we start. I once
saw cotton silt and snow float
in the sky at the same time. God said,
This is everything. I watched until
the sky became clear again instead
of dotted with all the happiness
the world contained and all my sorrow
that didn't know where else to go.

Walk-In Emergencies Welcome

I live in minefields, study dioramas
of disaster, pose in crime scenes. I pay
attention. Last night, I overheard a woman
in a restaurant complain that her friend always
confuses *Nothing is better with Better than
nothing.* I once rented an apartment near
a clinic with a sign that declared *Walk-in
Emergencies Welcome,* a consolation
of which I never availed myself. Nothing
can be better, the numbness a relief even
if the lack of feeling indicates danger
in a triage situation. What can I say? I've
always ignored *Do Not Enter Signs.* Brave, stupid,
willful? It all depends on the ending. Let's face it,
this game should have been mercied a long time ago.

Overheard, or This Is Not *Nighthawks*

I'm watching *The Biggest Loser*
in a Jack in the Box by the freeway.
How I got here, well, your guess is
as good as mine. Alone, I listen
to a woman on television crying while
a haggard-looking mom hands off her son
to his father for the weekend. Someone
near me says, *Seeing this show always*
makes me want to get really fat so I can
do something remarkable. I laugh despite
myself while police lights illuminate a cop
handcuffing a man who seems like he's been
through this routine. I slump in my booth
next to a sign that says, *We Don't Make It*
Until You Order It adorned with the clown
I remember from childhood, announcing,
Jack's Back! Somehow, I knew he would be.

Arson

Fires burned behind every window
in my first-grade assignment to draw
a house. Fifteen suns blazed in the sky,
and strange flowers bloomed in the yard
where children didn't play. *Who lives
in your house?* the teacher asked me.
Nobody lives there. Curlicues of smoke
streamed from the multiple chimneys.
I didn't include a door. Someone else
might have made up a story that included
a dramatic rescue. In my story the fires
always burned. The why didn't matter. I
only knew what I saw when I closed my eyes.

Half-Life

I wait as time makes the objects
of use into artifacts. They become
interesting, reminders of a past life
that continues as if time meant nothing,
meant everything. Forgive me if I misuse
your metaphysics. The sum is less
than the parts, and the story I tell
only fragments, each one saying, *I must
go, but I'll be back. It will be as if I
never left.* The dried flowers won't die
because they're already dead.

Look What You Created

"People are trapped in history and history is trapped in them."
James Baldwin

The year I almost died, I watched Rodney King
on *Celebrity Rehab with Dr. Drew*, Rodney's plea
from years earlier ringing in my ears, *Can't we all
just get along?* As I watched the City of Angels burn
in a morphine haze, I remembered the Devil himself
was the brightest angel. In the footage, the dead
and injured looked like shadows, the news cameras
trained on the flames. Alone in ICU, I couldn't tell
if it was day or night but I knew Rodney, watched
as he talked to Dr. Drew about the tape, the one where
the cops beat him on what seemed to be an endless loop.

Rodney drowned to death in his fiancé's pool
a few years later. He'd been trying to drown himself
from the inside with alcohol, to kill the pain bigger
than himself. That's what I imagine anyway, having
killed a bit of pain myself. I cried, thinking how sweet
Rodney had seen me through those hospital hours,
a tube down my throat, my blood contaminated
by the poison I'd carried inside of me until it exploded.
That's my story, and maybe that's everyone's story.

Color Your World

If I were a paint chip, I'd be Detroit
Gray, the color of winter, of cement,
of snow streaked with tire marks. I'd
be the color that you don't notice even
though it surrounds you. Nobody would
use me to lighten up a room. I'd be
the chip you'd put aside in favor of one
that forced you to pay attention, one
that spoke of possibility. I'm your unfinished
basement, the one you've been meaning
to renovate for all tomorrow's parties. I am
what exists for now, a shade over which you
would paint if only you could find the time.

Stop Me If You've Heard This One Before

Sometimes the world is so beautiful
I could just die, and then there are other
times like when I hear a story about a cop
who got called out on a domestic. No one
answered the door. He glanced around the yard,
mistaking a dead woman impaled on a fence
for a Halloween decoration, a bloody scarecrow.
Can you imagine the grief he took at the station?
someone asks. *All too well*, I say. Sometimes I'm
the woman, dolled up like a decoy designed to scare.
These guises lure and repel, leaving me hollow,
a projection for others to interpret. And sometimes
I'm the cop, missing what's right in front of me,
the shadows overpowering the light. As for the man
who left his wife to bleed out, I can't speak for him.
He made his point. Now I make mine. Fuck this shit.

The Arsenic Hour

Light leeches from the room
and there is no magic, only
evening and its sadness, the relief
of a day done followed by the realization
of another to come, that is, if you are
lucky. A psychic once told me, *Life*
gives you stunning luck in times
of danger, but day by day, your luck
sucks. And you talk in your sleep, he said,
a sign of mediumship. The dead speak
through you. But your own voice is muffled,
drowned out by laundry, dishes, an office
where you are always busy and nothing
gets done. You hear a siren, the predictable
emergencies of the night. Don't ask.

In the Terminal

Sometimes I still wait for my dad
to land, my childhood a dream
from which I can't quite wake. Years
later, he still taught ground school,
still took students for their first flights.
A student flew into a power line,
their plane exploding into flames,
both dead before the ashes consumed
the ground. Someone called to tell me,
from the tiny orange terminal, the place
I had spent all those childhood Saturdays,
reading books and dreaming of big cities,
while my dad made extra money to pay
my mother's medical bills. People talk
about when flying was glamorous,
when beautiful women presented you
meals under bell jars. I never travelled
that way. Instead, I rode in the luggage
area of a Cessna, stowed away, a carry-on
that he never forgot to take with him.

How to Make Your Own Bed

It starts with a joke
Four nails and some wood
Nobody said it would be comfortable
Lying and sleeping are optional.

Endless Summer

The Beach Boys sing *Surfin' USA*
as my dad blows up a raft so my
sister and I can take turns standing
on it in the pool until we lose balance.
My dad, more handsome than any
Beach Boy, pulled me out of this pool
when I was three. Fully clothed, lit
cigarette dangling from his mouth, he
dove and arose out of the water to never
smoke again. In this Polaroid memory,
he never fades. It's summer, you see,
and the light stays for so long that
everyone can go surfing, and you forget
that even the longest days fade into night.

The Lady or the Tiger? Capture Them Both

Nobody wants to hear this.
What luck! I don't want to say it.
We stop at perfect days that shall
linger without form. There's no
shaking this premonition that I've
been here before, the road travelled
by way too many. What can I say?
For my next trick, I'll need a volunteer.

Obey the Night

Three doors down, there's a crack house
guarded by pit bulls. The poisons I prefer
are legal. You can't pick who you love.
The streets talk to me, but nobody knows
my name. I read about the famous dead
while ignoring my own burial grounds.
It's bad luck to build near a cemetery
so I carry mine with me. My purse
empties to feed my wants. Night
protects me from you but not myself.

This Painting Is Part of Our Permanent Collection

You wake to the accident of your life.
Your dreamt that none of this ever happened,
that the dead didn't really die, that fire never
burned, the results came back negative. Relief
floods you until you open your eyes, return
to your old house. The key you left under the rock
so long it left an imprint in the dirt is gone. You'll
have to break a window. You are willing to inflict
damage. Whoever is calling will have to wait. Don't
worry. Nothing has changed except the locks.

I Am the Fist

There will be no tears.
You will forget how
to cry. You never cry
but you always look
like you're about to be hit.
You cringe at the sound
of your own voice, the way
it betrays you. People mistake
your silence for strength.
Of course, you stopped believing
there was something to admire
a long time ago. You didn't ask
for this. You don't ask for anything
at all. By you, I mean me. But you
knew that all along, didn't you?

Exclusions May Apply

There's something, he said, *about the way*
she loves me then doesn't. She's a cold,
beautiful city that I've only seen on posters.
I laughed and said, *And I thought I was*
the poet. He smiled, the kind of smile
a doctor offers you before a terminal diagnosis.
You've never been in love with someone
who doesn't love you. I shake my head, try
to sympathize. But nothing is ever enough,
and we both agree, that's the problem. *We're too old*
for this shit, he adds, wondering if he should call
her. I tell him that nobody calls anyone these days.
It's all text. *Is it late enough for a drink?* he asks.
I say what I always do, *Where's the harm?* It's
always late enough. Maybe it just seems like it
should be late enough somewhere, anywhere.

You Are the Camera

I shoot in available light as if
there were no other options. I used
to take pictures of accidents. Now
I take pictures of myself, the crime
scene. I tamper with the evidence,
sleight of hand the only trick I know.
You offer to help, but I can't take it.
You can't walk across these hot coals,
no matter what story you tell yourself.

Where the Negatives Are Buried

The city recedes until even
this receding leaves me.
I know from that one story
that no one can reside in paradise
forever and that paradise only reveals
itself as such in the rearview
mirror. This space between what
was and what is, this purgatory,
I do not leave it. I cannot let
the dead bury the dead. I become
the negative of a picture, one
I never allow myself to develop.

Trick and Treat

We all agreed to this, and yet
it seems like a mirage, the streets full
of costumed children. The Mets are
losing the fourth game of the World
Series, and I can't help but feel
the pain of the faithful fans watching
defeat snatched from the hands of victory
once again. Tonight parents instruct
their children to take candy from strangers.
And on this one night a year, I answer
the door without hesitation, unafraid
of the ghouls that greet me. In the midst
of inevitable defeat, the rules don't apply.

Take, Lock, Hide

I didn't change the locks
and the video camera records
without tape. If there was a fire,
I wouldn't know what to save.
I took the batteries out of the smoke
detector. The sounds on the street
have ceased to mean anything other
than that I am alive enough to know
danger, headed toward me like
overnight guests that have let me
know they are on their way.

Straight No Chaser

I once visited a church
where a preacher claimed
we could drink poison without
harm, provided our faith never
waivered. *Drink from the living
water,* he says. *You will never
suffer again.* I knew a woman
who drank Kamikazes, lime juice
and vodka, with a name that invokes
missions slated to end with certain
death. Does self-inflicted pain hurt less?
Only if you don't count the mantra,
You did this to yourself, persistent
as you wish the obliteration would be.

Vacation Bible School

Before the puppet show, Melissa and I split
a stolen Valium. As the children gathered,
a dreamy feeling descended on the eighth
grade me, benevolence for all I saw—the cheap
hand puppets, a mouse and giraffe who
became Jonah and the whale. I put my mouse
into the mouth of Melissa's giraffe while God
waited for Jonah to get himself right. He'd
run from Ninevah only to suffer. Brother
Buddy complimented us on our performance,
telling me that longsuffering was my fruit
of the spirit. I didn't sound good, even medicated
against harm and boredom. I didn't know then
that you didn't have to be swallowed whole,
that you could swallow the whale and not
know you were trapped by what was inside you.

The City of God

Do not look behind you.
You cannot sing the songs
of Zion in a foreign land.
Do not tell anyone of what
you used to be. I once heard
a rumor of a girl who kept
her used sanitary napkins
in a dresser drawer, preservation
instinct gone awry. Cast into
the future, I wonder about her,
what happened to all that dried blood.

These Streets

You never know where to turn.
Snow falls, dirty before it hits
the ground. Liquor stores surround
me, escape and salvation if only for
a bit before the predictable darkness
takes all. The house always wins,
no matter how long you've lived in it.
A car passes decorated with a bumper sticker
that proclaims *Freedom Isn't Free.*
In the window of a burnt-out house,
Someone has put up a political poster
that says *Progress.* Graffiti tells me
nothing, just bright spots of color
that haven't yet worn down. I wish
I knew where I was. But, of course, I do.

Technicolor

You have been at this party for a while.
The candles have collapsed on themselves,
the napkins ball like fists. and you can no
longer pretend you have somewhere else to go/
The sequins on your dress that once caught
the light have dulled over time. When did your
life become sepia? You pretend nothing has
faded, that the best is yet to come. After all,
you've put on your party dress, your game face,
your brave face, the one that feels like stone.
And you remember when you and everything
else sparkled, lit up like wondrous Technicolor.

Pretty in A Hard Way

The ground moves with snakes,
and the sky bleeds red streaks,
as if the night couldn't leave
without a fight, and all your dreams
are tragedies where no one dies,
but everyone suffers. In your past
life when you woke up hungover, you'd
think, *Anything is better than this.*

You were a confection, a little
dead around the eyes, the kind
of woman people describe as
pretty in a hard way. And you
refuse to go gently into that good
night. And let's face it. Not all
of them were good ones. You don't
care. There is nothing you can do
about it now. Gather the pieces
as best you can even if they cut you.

At the Crossroads of the Dying World

There's a mall cop perched atop
a Segway, riding an escalator,
and I marvel at this strange sight
near the food court. Florescent
lights onto shuttered stores dotted
with anchors that have been here
since I was a child. I drift to the playground
where exhausted parents stare at their cell
phones or into the distance while their
children scream and jump and cry
on plastic toys designed to look like animals.

I watch the scene, wishing I could stop time
and its relentless march over us all, wishing
I could close my eyes and will the B. Daltons
back into existence. So many things used
to be something else. I look at a jewelry
repair shop which used to be a novelty store
that sold small trees coated with gold. I'd always
wanted one. The mall cop rides past me, back
to the escalator, and I see my entire life cascade,
like the motorized stairs in their endless loop.
The trees with golden leaves that had once
beckoned me with their promises
of glamour, such as it was, are still gone.

The Show Must Go On

This past I carry feels heavy,
but when exposed, it evaporates
into the dust of nothing. I am
a magician, my strange alchemy
turns that which seems solid
into thin air. What can I say?
I write to you in invisible ink.

Acknowledgments

If You're Drinking to Forget, Please Pay in Advance—*Threepenny Review*
 Imprisoned Lightning—Quiddity
Enchantment Ballroom—*Circle Show*
Smart, Very Smart—*Delmarva Review*
Strike Anywhere—*Helen*
Applebee's Hotel Bar—Boca Raton, Florida—*520 Magazine*
That's Not A Window, It's A Mirror—*Vending Machine Press*
The Saint of This Used to Be—*Ibis Head Review*
Three Mile Island at Night—*Vending Machine Press*
The Bride of Frankenstein—*Taj Mahal Review*
Vision—*2 River Review*
The Bronx Is Burning—*Olegtany Review*
San Francisco, Dusk, Pre-Millennium—*Nerve Cowboy*
Watch What Develops—*Litbreak*
Where Good Things Come Easy—*Olegtany Review*
Esoterica—*Atlanta Review*
Flamethrower—*Apeiron Review*
If I Seem Free, It's Because I'm Always Running—*Tenpenny Review*
The Priestess of the Imperial Cult—*Ibis Head Review*
The Year in Review—*Ibis Head Review*
Possum Kingdom Lake—*The Lake*
The Judgment of Heaven—*The American Journal of Poetry*
Stock Footage—*Delmarva Review*
Obituary for A Neon Angel—*Delmarva Review*
Blank Inside for Your Message—*Third Wednesday*
Walk-In Emergencies Welcome—*Litbreak*
Overheard, or This Is Not Nighthawks—*Olegtany Review*
Arson—*Badlands Literary Journal*
Half-Life—*Rock and Sling*
Color Your World—*Hotel Amerika*
Stop Me If You've Heard This One Before—*Cholla Needles*
How to Make Your Own Bed—*TXTOBJ*
In the Terminal—*KSOV Review*
The Lady or the Tiger? Capture Them Both—*Hamilton Stone Review*
Obey the Night—*Hamilton Stone Review*
This Painting Is Part of Our Permanent Collection—*Eclectica Magazine*
I Am the Fist—*Hamilton Stone Review*

Exclusions May Apply—*Dime Show Review*
You Are the Camera—*The Binnacle Review*
Where the Negatives Are Buried—*Third Wednesday*
Trick or Treat—*Hotel Amerika*
Take, Lock, Hide—*Easy Street*
Straight No Chaser—*Flint Hills Review*
Vacation Bible School—*Big Windows Review*
The City of God—*2 River Review*
These Streets—*Blue Collar Review*
Technicolor—*Clementine Review*
At the Crossroads of the Dying World—Red Weather
The Show Must Go On—*Nerve Cowboy*

Michelle Brooks grew up in Mineral Wells, Texas, a small town on the edge of west Texas. Her work has been published in *Threepenny Review, Hayden's Ferry Review, Iowa Review, Gargoyle, Alaska Quarterly Review, Hotel Amerika*, and elsewhere. She has published a collection of poetry, *Make Yourself Small,* (Backwaters Press), and a novella, *Dead Girl, Live Boy,* (Storylandia Press).

One of her first jobs working for the Mineral Wells Index inspired an interest in photography. Given her complete inexperience with a camera, she learned how to take pictures and develop them in the dark room after ruining many rolls of film. Her photographs have appeared in *Shadows and Light, Alchemy, Literary Heist*, and elsewhere. Upon graduating from the University of North Texas, she moved to Detroit, Michigan, her favorite city.